DATE			

THE LEGAL GUIDE TO MOTHER GOOSE

TRANSLATED BY DON SANDBURG

PRICE/STERN/SLOAN
Publishers, Inc., Los Angeles

Text Copyright ©1978 by Don Sandburg
Illustrations Copyright © 1978 by Price/Stern/Sloan Publishers, I
Published by Price/Stern/Sloan Publishers, Inc.
410 North La Cienega Boulevard, Los Angeles, California 900
Printed in the United States of America
ISBN: 0-8431-0480-5

TABLE OF CONTENTS

INTRODUCTION

ungsters have enjoyed Mother Goose Rhymes for gen-
tions. Parents have read them aloud to their children
h equal pleasure. But what about lawyers? They are
en parents themselves. Do they — indeed, can they
recite these delightful ditties to their children verbatim?
e answer, of course, is an unequivocal NO! Nor could
y be expected to, since the Rhymes are written in a
gue totally foreign to their unique intellect.

re, for the first time, is a proper translation for
wyers. Now, they too, may understand, enjoy and
ite to their children these inspiring messages in their
n strange tongue.

Jack and Jill

Went up the hill

To fetch a pail of water

"JACK AND JILL"

Accident Report

The party of the first part hereinafter

known as Jack . . . and . . .

The party of the second part hereinafter

known as Jill . . .

Ascended or caused to be ascended an

elevation of undetermined height and

degree of slope, hereinafter referred to

as "hill."

Whose purpose it was to obtain, attain,

procure, secure, or otherwise, gain

acquisition to, by any and/or all means

available to them a receptacle or con-

tainer, hereinafter known as "pail,"

Jack fell down

And broke his crown

suitable for the transport of a liquid

whose chemical properties shall be

limited to hydrogen and oxygen, the

proportions of which shall not be less

than or exceed two parts for the first

mentioned element and one part for the

latter. Such combination will

hereinafter be called "water."

On the occasion stated above, it has bee

established beyond reasonable doubt tha

Jack did plunge, tumble, topple, or

otherwise be caused to lose his footing

in a manner that caused his body to be

thrust into a downward direction.

As a direct result of these combined

And Jill came tumbling after.

circumstances, Jack suffered fractures and contusions of his cranial regions. Jill, whether due to Jack's misfortune or not, was known to also tumble in similar fashion after Jack. (Whether the term, "after," shall be interpreted in a spatial or time passage sense, has not been determined.)

Wee Willie Winkie runs
through the town.

Upstairs, downstairs in
his nightgown.

Rapping at the windows, crying
through the lock.

Are the children all in bed

"WILLIE WINKIE"

Indictment

The defendant, known as Wee Willie

Winkie, has been observed speeding

in a congested area, thereby, vio-

lating Section 22350 of the Vehicle

Code.

He has further been cited

under Section 311 of the Penal Code

for indecent exposure and is

additionally accused of

violating Sections 602 and 647 of the

Penal Code for trespassing and dis-

orderly conduct.

We, nevertheless, request that the

for now it's eight o'clock.

6	court grant clemency in respect to
.7	the above charges in view of the
.8	defendant's conscientious efforts
19	in helping to enforce the mis-
20	demeanor statute of the Municipal
21	Code dealing with the nocturnal
22	curfew for juveniles.

There was an old woman
who lived in a shoe
She had so many children she
didn't know what to do.

She gave them some broth
without any bread.

She whipped them all soundly
and put them to bed.

"THE OLD WOMAN IN THE SHOE"

Verdict

An elderly female, surname unknown,
residing in a foot-like dwelling, has – due
to an ignorance of birth control – become
the bearer of so many progeny that the
subsequent burden caused her undue hard
ship, resulting in anxiety and frustration.
The siblings' sustenance consisted of an
attenuated nutrient liquid unaccompanied
by any baked cereal products. She was
found guilty of aggravated assault and
child abuse and is now serving twenty
years in a correctional institution for
unfit mothers.

Jack Spratt could eat no fat

His wife could eat no lean.

And so between them both,
you see

They licked the platter clean.

"JACK SPRATT"

Divorce Agreement

Whereas Jack Spratt, hereinafter

called the respondent, is incapable

of ingesting fatty substance,

And whereas his spouse, hereinafter

referred to as the petitoner, is

unable to consume any lean tissue,

it is hereby ordered that the

respondent and the petitioner shall,

as equals, between them . . .

share and completely dispose of all

mutually owned edible meat products

according to their separate and in-

dividual protein preference.

What are little boys made of?

What are little boys made of?

Frogs and snails

"BOYS AND GIRLS"

Medical Findings

COUNSELOR: Doctor, in laymen's terms, could you describe the physiological makeup of the young male homo sapiens?

COUNSELOR: I'll rephrase the question. What would you consider, in your expert opinion, to be the basic components of the average male adolescent?

DOCTOR: To the best of our medical knowledge, the most vital organs consist of tail-like amphibia and gastropod mollusks . . .

And puppy dog tails

hat's what little boys are made of.

What are little girls made of?

What are little girls made of?

Sugar and spice

DOCTOR: And minute traces of the

rear appendages of young members of

the Canis familiaris species.

COUNSELOR: Is that it?

DOCTOR: Yes, Sir.

COUNSELOR: Let's talk about the

female gender. How are they

biologically structured?

COUNSELOR: Let me repeat that.

What, in your professional opinion,

are the most essential life-

sustaining ingredients of the young

human female?

DOCTOR: As a psychologist, I'd have to

say their most abundant components

And all things nice.

are sucrose and dried aromatic

vegetable substances and . . .

COUNSELOR: Yes, doctor . . .

DOCTOR: And all things nice.

COUNSELOR: Really, Miss Jones . . .

I mean, Doctor Jones . . . Isn't

that a rather sexist attitude?

Fee, Fi, Fo, Fum

I smell the blood of an
Englishman.

"THE GIANT"

The Confession

Legal jargon meaning, "Retainer,"

or "Fee up front."

I hereby declare, assert, affirm

attest, proclaim, state and avow,

that on the occasion in question,

I did indeed detect with my

olfactory senses a scent, odorous

essence, pungency or emanation that

strongly suggested the presence of blood

and further arrived at a reasonable

determination that the said blood in

question was that of a loyal subject of

the English crown, its colonies or

Be he alive or be he dead

I'll grind his bones to
make my bread.

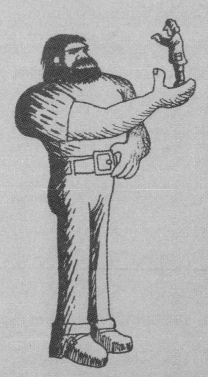

holdings.

The question of whether the aforesaid

is living or deceased has not yet

been determined.

It is in any case my intention with

malice and forethought and pre-

meditation to cause his skeletal

anatomy to be pulverized for the

purpose of using the resulting

residue for my baking needs.

I hereby inscribe my name on

the 12th day of September, 1842.

Yours very truly,

the Giant

Roses are red

"ROSES ARE RED"

Rebuttal

The statement that "roses are red"

implies that all members of the

botanical family, Rosaceal,

can be no other color.   This

is clearly a fallacious and

erroneous assumption in view

of the fact that the genus,

Rosa, containing more than

one hundred (100) species, is found in

a multitude of tinctures including,

but not limited to, ochet,

magenta, heliotrope, vermillion

and sunset violet.   This observa-

Violets are blue

Sugar is sweet

tion can be supported, if need be,
by the expert testimony of horti-
culturalists and elderly female persons.
Similarly, the generalization that
all flowers of the genus, <u>Viola,</u> are
blue can be refuted in view
of the fact that the existence of
other hues for the 400 known
species can be documented by
witnesses of reputable expertise
in the field of violetology   (i.e.
the yellow pansy violet or ped-
unculata that flourish in the Great
Plains area.)
Although it has been established

And so are you.

beyond a reasonable doubt that

the organic compound $C_{12} H_{22} O_{11}$,

in most cases, will leave a saccharine

taste on one's palate...

We, nevertheless, cannot presume

the validity of the concluding state-

ment. Construed in a literal sense,

we must infer that such assertion,

"and so are you," is intended to mean

that a person tastes sweet, when in

point of actual fact, there is no

evidential substantiation of the gustatory

evaluation of the human species.

Humpty Dumpty sat on a wall

Humpty Dumpty had a great fall

All the king's horses and all
the king's men

Couldn't put Humpty Dumpty
back together again.

"HUMPTY DUMPTY" / Inquest

An ovum known as H. Dumpty, hereinafte

referred to as "Humpty" was postured

in a perched position on a partition.

The aforementioned suffered a

sudden descent, not of his own

volition.

The Marshalling Forces of his

Majesty's resources, specifically

those of Equus Caballus and male

homo sapien origin . . .

were incapable of reconstructing

and/or reassembling Humpty's original

status quo.

Tweedle-dum and Tweedle-dee

Resolved to have a battle

For Tweedle-dum said
Tweedle-dee

Had spoiled his nice new rattle

Just then flew by a monstrous
crow

As big as a tar barrel

"TWEEDLE-DUM AND TWEEDLE DEE'

Reconciliation

Tweedle-dum and Tweedle-dee

did mutually agree to engage in a

hostile confrontation,

as a result of Tweedle-dee's accusation

. . . that Tweedle-dum

had maliciously and without provocation

or forethought devastated his noise-

making device.

At this given point in time, however,

a prodigious Corvus brachyrhychos,

whose proportions approximated that of

a receptacle commonly used for the

containment of viscous hydrocarbons,

Which frightened both the
heroes so

They quite forgot their quarrel.

landed in the immediate vicinity.

The spectacle of which filled the two

intrepid opponents with such

terror and consternation that . . .

They quickly sought a state of detente.

There was a crooked man

And he walked a crooked mile

He found a crooked sixpence

Against a crooked stile

He bought a crooked cat

Which caught a crooked mouse

And they all lived together

In a little crooked house

"THE CROOKED MAN"

Surveillance Report

The criminal suspect was observed

ambulating while under the influence of

alcohol. Said subject was further

noted to uncover some counter-

feit adjacent to a dilapidated stair-

case. He procured a fraudulent feline

who, in turn, apprehended a miscreant

member of the rodent species, Mus

musculus, after which

they collectively formed a commune

in a small structure used for purposes

of ill repute.

43

Mary had a little lamb

With fleece as white as snow

And everywhere that Mary went

The lamb was sure to go
It followed her to school one day

"MARY HAD A LITTLE LAMB"

Police Report

The subject, a female caucasian, hereinafter known as Mary, surname unknown,
has been frequently observed in the close
company of an immature member of
the Bovidae family . . .
whose remarkable floccuent albino
surface resembles frozen precipitation
in the form of hexagonal snow crystals.
It appears that regardless of Mary's
migratory habits, the woolly
juvenile maintained pursuance.
Such pursuit of the suspect led the
unfledged species of the genus, Ovis,

That was quite against the rule

It made the children laugh
and play

To see a lamb at school.

to the subject's institute of learning --

Which is a violation of Section 63.55

of the Municipal Code.

The subject's academic peers subse-

quently engaged in exultation, jubila-

tion, frolic and general rejoicing

at the incongruous apparition of a

callow member of the Hollow Horn

Ruminant family at a place of aca-

demia.

Peter, Peter, Pumpkin Eater

Had a wife and couldn't keep her

He put her in a pumpkin shell

And there he kept her very well.

"PETER"

Sentence

Peter, (alias Peter), known for his peculiar propensity for the consumption of a variety of squash known colloquially as pumpkin, was in possession of a spouse who was a compulsive fugitive. He imprisoned her within the confines of a shell from a fruit of Curcurbita pepo, where she is now serving time under maximum security.

Hush-A-Bye Baby,
Upon the tree top

When the wind blows,
The cradle will rock

When the bough breaks,
The cradle will fall

"HUSH-A-BYE BABY"

Order of the Court

It shall be deemed mandatory for the infant in question to desist and refrain from vocal demonstrations while reposing in the uppermost regions of said tree.

The climatic conditions are such as to effect winds of such nature and to such extent that they will create an oscillating movement in the sleeping accommodation of said infant.

Such meteorological conditions shall induce the fracturing of the branch supporting said facility thereby

Down will come cradle,
Baby and all.

ultimately causing the rapid descent of same.

There shall be a downward plunge of the sleeping apparatus, bringing with it the reposed infant perilously contained within, along with all objects, para-phenalia, and debris directly related to the above-mentioned items.

"BAA BAA BLACK SHEEP"

Last Will and Testament

I, being of sound and disposing mind and

memory, not acting under duress, menac

fraud, or the undue influence of any pers

or persons whatsoever, do hereby make,

publish, and declare this to be my last

will and testament, hereby revoking all

wills and heretofore made by me, and giv

devise and bequeath the residue of my est

and all my earthly possessions consisting

in whole of my three bags full of wool in

the following manner:

    a. One for The Master

    b. One for the Dame.

c. One for the little boy

who lives down the lane

Signed on the <u>8th</u> day of <u>August</u>, 19<u>76</u>

1 | **Early to Bed   Early to rise**

2 | **Makes a man . . .**

3 | **HEALTHY,** Well, Sound, Hearty, Hale,

4 | Hardy, Wholesome, Florid, Robust,

5 | Vital, Salubrious, Vigorous, Uninfectio

6 | Unscathed and Hygenic . . .

7 | **WEALTHY,** Rich, Affluent, Opulent,

8 | Moneyed, Luxurious, Well-To-Do,

9 | Financially Secure, Monitarily Endowe

10 | Prosperous, Well-Capitalized, Numis-

11 | matically Stable, Amply Resourced,

12 | Solvent, Generously Funded, and Well-

Provided . . .

WISE, Sagacious, Learned, Profound,

Deep, Judicious, Knowing, Cognitive, Well-

Advised, Aware, Perceptive, Apprised,

Erudite, Scholarly, Instructed, Informed,

Lettered, Educated, Enlightened, Shrewd,

Well-Grounded, Scholastic, Accomplished,

Omniscient, Intellectual, Academic, Know-

able, Astute, Discerning, Discreet,

Prudent, Articulate, Conscious, and

Cognizant . . .

To name a few

Peter Piper picked a peck of
pickled peppers;

A peck of pickled peppers
Peter Piper picked.

If Peter Piper picked a peck
of pickled peppers,

Where's the peck of pickled
peppers Peter Piper picked?

"PETER PIPER"

Cross Examination By

The Counsel For The

Prosecution

OBVIOUSLY SELF-EXPLANATORY.

Hickory Dickory Dock

The mouse ran up the clock.

The clock struck one

"HICKORY DICKORY DOCK"

Recess

This court is now recessed

for lunch.